WHAT
COLOR
ARE YOU?

A Fanciful Journey of Biblical Truth and Reality

I0098734

Robert E. Daley

The Larry Czerwonka Company, LLC
Hilo, Hawaiʻi

First Edition — December 2015

This book is set in 14-point Garamond

Published by: The Larry Czerwonka Company, LLC
http://czerwonkapublishing.com

Printed in the United States of America

ISBN: 0692597964
ISBN-13: 978-0692597965

All scriptures used in this work are taken from the King James Version of the Scriptures.

BOOKS BY ROBERT E. DALEY

WHAT
COLOR

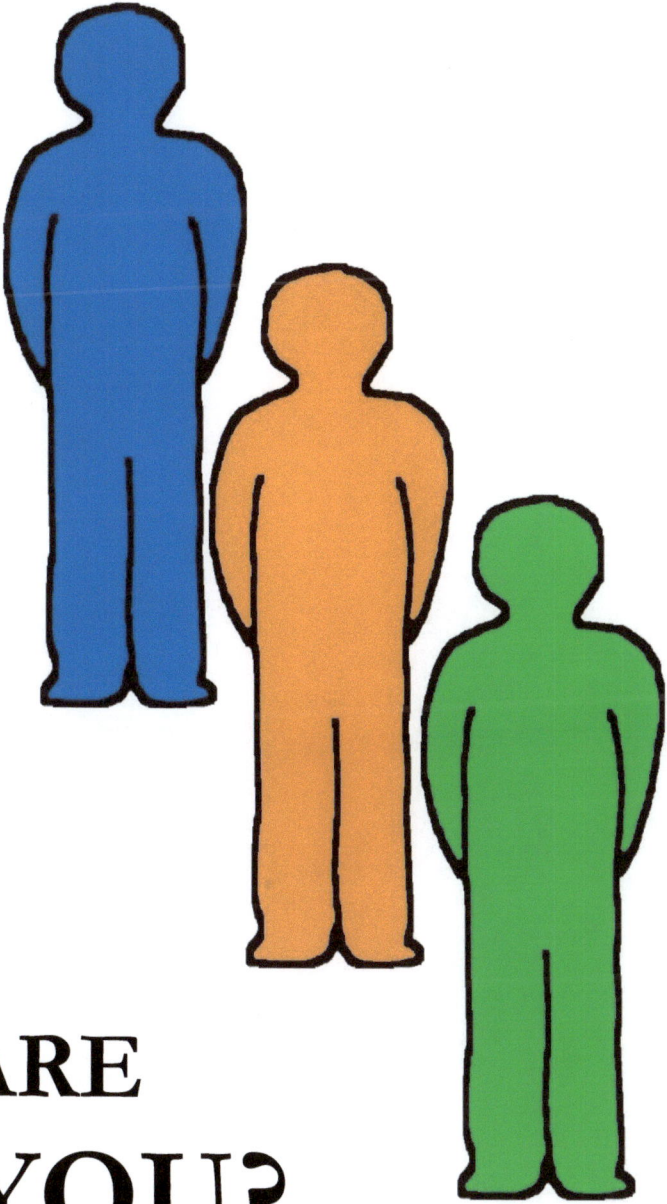

ARE
YOU?

Introduction

This little work is intended to present a clear and simple explanation of the stark and yet genuine differences between being a pagan Gentile, or an Abrahamic Covenant Jewish individual, or a brand new, New Creature in Christ Jesus.

By the use of color to distinguish each group, it makes the explanation much clearer.

Within the Christian world today there is a lot of confusion as to what each of these *groups* are and what makes them so different from one another.

The author also desires that all persons receive a complete understanding as to what happens to any individual when they ask Jesus of Nazareth to forgive them of their sins, and come into their heart and life.

Written in a style to be understood by adults and children alike, please read this simple presentation of God's plan for each of His Human creations.

What Color Are You?

The plan that God has for Mankind is in many respects beyond words. His love is more than we are ever able to measure, because the Scriptures reveal to us that God does not simply have love, but rather *is* Love. His capacity for mercy and grace and forgiveness and compassion and goodness are without boundaries.

God's holy Word, in giving unto us all things that pertain to life and Godliness *(II Peter 1:3)*, reveals to us the wonderful Master Plan that He has established from everlasting for men and women to be restored in their relationship to Him. And God is a God of faith. He created this whole universe that we find ourselves a part of . . . by faith. And that is the way that He operates in everything.

For some people what God has done seems clear, and they just move right along in their walk with the Lord. For others, the Scriptures present the facts of what God has done, but they do not seem to grasp with simplicity the clarity of the picture.

With the help of the Holy Spirit of God, we shall take a look at the facts from another perspective, using colors in a simple illustration, and trust God to give unto us insight and confirmation. For the purpose of this illustration, we will use the color blue to represent all pagan Gentiles, and the color orange to represent all Abrahamic Covenant Jewish individuals, and the color green to represent all New Creatures, i.e., all Born-Again Christians.

How It All Began . . .

Within the Book of Genesis, which is the first book of the Bible, we discover that God created Man *in* His own image, and *after* His own likeness *(Genesis 1:26)*. With the original intent that all men and women would be God's very own children, and that He would finally have the family that He has always desired.

Adam and Eve were full of life, and some people believe that they literally glowed with the light of God that lived within them. The Scriptures go on to tell us that Sin entered into the picture, and when Adam and Eve disobeyed God and fell prey to Sin, they were separated from God and actually became subjects of the author of Sin, who was the Devil.

When this occurred, for the sake of our illustration, may we see this as the point in time when men and women changed color to the color blue.

Adam was blue. Eve was blue. And when their children were born, they were all born blue. God was not able to talk to His men anymore the way that He used to. He still loved men, and He had established a Plan to restore His men to a position of son-ship; but for now, all of the people who were born as descendants of Adam and Eve were all born blue.

Blue men began to build cities. Blue men began to call upon the name of the Lord. Some blue women were tricked and seduced by evil fallen angels and produced unredeemable offspring. And one blue man was even translated from off of this Earth so that he should not experience physical death for thousands of years.

Wickedness continued to increase more and more on the Earth as men went deeper and deeper into Sin. The unredeemable offspring of the blue women and evil fallen angels also continued to increase. The darkness got so bad that God was going to have to do something about it, so He called on a blue man to build a large boat in which he might save his family. And God flooded the Earth with water. When the flood was over, the blue man and his blue wife and blue children left the boat and began to fill up the Earth again with blue people.

Some of the blue people remembered God, but many of them forgot Him and began to worship everything else under the sun except the One True God. All of the blue people even came together and began to build a huge tower to challenge the Living God. So God came down from heaven and confused their speech and scattered the people to different parts of the land.

The people were no longer of one language, but they were all still blue. They wandered to all of the different parts of the land and built many towns and cities. At a point in time, God broke up the land into several pieces and some of the people were separated from each other by water. Still, they continued to increase and blue people began to fill up the Earth all over the place.

God Begins To Put His Plan Into Action . . .

About four hundred and thirty years after the Flood of Noah was over, a blue baby boy was born and his father named him Abram. Abram grew up to be a fine young man and he had several admirable qualities about him. One day God approached Abram and told him that He wanted to establish a legal contract with him and make him His partner. God said that He would protect him, and provide for him, and fight for him, and make him rich, and cause that he would have many, many descendants. Abram figured that this was a pretty good deal, and so he agreed to enter into this legal contract with God called a Covenant. Part of the deal was that Abram would have his named changed to Abraham, and he and all of his male descendants would have to become circumcised as a sign of this Covenant.

When the contract was finalized and Abraham was circumcised, something wonderful happened . . . he changed from the color blue to the color orange. He was no longer a blue man. He was no longer the same as all of the other blue men around him. He was in a legal relationship with the Living God and he was different. Abraham's wife also changed to the color orange and they were very excited about all of the orange people that would now come forth because of God's promise to cause that Abraham would have many, many descendants.

When God established His Plan to restore man, He knew it would only work if it were based upon faith. And when year after year went by and Abraham and his wife did not have any children, they decided to *help God out* by using one of the blue servant girls named Hagar to produce a son.

This was not part of God's Plan. This new blue baby boy was **not** the fulfillment of the promise that God had made . . . faith was not involved!

One day God visited Abraham and told him that the promise that He had made unto him to make him a father was going to come to pass the very next year. Abraham was now an old man and he laughed at God's statement. But he still believed that if **anybody** could do it, God could. So, Abraham trusted in God, and sure enough the next year his wife Sarah gave birth to a bouncing blue baby boy! According to rules of the Covenant, this baby boy needed to be circumcised, and when he was something wonderful happened . . . he changed color from blue to orange.

And as that boy grew up and got married he had two sons. And when his boys were circumcised, they changed from blue to orange. And so it continued down through the centuries. Orange people increased more and more.

God kept His promises and protected His orange *partner* people. He provided for them. He made them rich. He kept them healthy. And whenever anyone tried to beat them up, He fought for them. The most precious of all of the things that God promised to do was . . . He promised to send them a man who was to be more *special* than any other man: A man who would one day become their king. The best king that they could ever have. A king who was wise. A king who was kind. A king who was strong . . . both physically and spiritually. A king who was unlike any other. He would be the Promised One. He would be the One, who would finally restore men to God. He would be the One, who would make it possible for men and women to become the children of God again. Through him, God would establish a new contract for those who wanted to be a part of His family. This new contract, just like the first one, would also have to work by faith.

God Keeps His Promise . . .

On a certain day, God sent one of His messenger angels to a young orange girl named Mary to tell her that He wanted her to be the one to bring His promised king into the world. She did not understand everything that was said, but because she loved God, she agreed to do it. And, on a certain special day another bouncing baby boy came into this world. He was circumcised according to God's rules and became wonderfully orange. God told the young girl to call his name Jesus.

Until he was two years old, Jesus grew up in a small town where most all of the people around him were orange. One day some blue men came to visit him and bring him some special gifts because they believed that he was a very important person. They talked about some things not being quite right with the current king of the orange people, and then they left to return home to their own land once again.

God spoke to Jesus' earthly father, in a dream, and told him to take his orange wife and orange son into a land filled with blue people, because there were those who wanted to kill Jesus, and to stay in that land until He called for him again. Jesus' earthly father agreed and the family went down into Egypt.

After the danger had passed, God called Jesus and his family back into the land of the orange people and directed them to live in a city named Nazareth. Orange Jesus grew and was liked by everyone who met him. He was a very obedient young man, and he stayed with his parents until he was thirty years of age.

After his thirtieth birthday, Jesus left home and began to go and tell all of the orange people that he was the *special* orange man that God had promised to send. He went into towns and villages near to where he grew up, as well as to cities that were far away in the land of the orange people. He gathered a close group of orange friends and shared with them what he had read in the Scriptures: that even though he was the *special* orange man that God had promised to send . . . the people were not going to believe him . . . faith was **not** involved! Most of his close friends believed in him, but not all. Even though they did not quite understand, they heard him tell of God's love. They heard him tell of God's goodness. They saw the special things that he did and knew that only God could do such things. They saw that there really was something special about him.

One night after Jesus and his friends had finished dinner, he was arrested by a group of blue men. Orange men who had come to hate Jesus and had said that they would not receive him as coming from God, complained to the blue sheriff and the sheriff sent his men to arrest Jesus. They held a kangaroo court and decided that Jesus should be put to death. He had not done anything wrong, but it was part of God's Plan.

They took the orange Jesus out to a hilltop and nailed him to a cross. With stripes from a beating, nails through his hands and feet, and a crown of thorns pressed upon his brow, Jesus died and went to Hell for you and for me. It was part of God's Plan.

Three days and three nights later, when the Scripture had been fulfilled and the price for Sin had been fully paid, the Living God raised up orange Jesus from the dead, (both spiritual and physical) and a wonderful thing happened . . . he changed color from orange to green.

All of heaven rejoiced as green Jesus was made the guest of honor at the party and sat down at the right hand of the Living God, as the newly begotten Son of the Highest. Faith was involved! Through the new green Jesus, God established His New Christian Covenant.

For forty days after he is raised from the dead, green Jesus appeared various times to his orange friends. One day as he met with several of them at dinner time, he said unto them "Receive ye the Holy Spirit." When he said this, he breathed on them and a wonderful thing happened . . . they all changed from the color orange to the color green! They were all so excited! It was part of God's Plan.

When it was time, green Jesus said goodbye to his new green friends and told them to go and tell everybody about God's Plan to restore men and make them His children. Several days later the green men and women were gathered together in the temple and there was a wonderful visitation of the Holy Spirit of God from heaven. During all of the commotion many orange men and orange women drew near to find out what was happening. The green men began to share with them God's Plan like Jesus had told them, and something wonderful happened . . . about three thousand orange people heard of God's Plan and believed, and changed from the color orange to the color green that very day. Faith was involved!

From that day forth green people began to go all over the town and tell orange people about God's Plan. Many orange people believed and changed from the color orange to the color green. Some orange people refused to believe God's Plan and so they remained orange. For some years, orange people everywhere heard about God's Plan. Some believed and changed to the color green, and others did not believe and they remained orange. Faith was not involved!

One day a green man named Peter was waiting for the lunch to be served. While he waited the Holy Spirit of God told him that some blue men were going to visit him and that he needed to go with them. The blue men said that they were sent to bring green Peter to see their blue boss. Green Peter and a couple of his green friends went with the blue men and when they reached their target destination green Peter began to tell the blue men about the Plan of God. As he spoke, the Holy Spirit of God moved upon the blue men and a wonderful thing happened . . . they changed from the color blue to the color green. Faith was involved! Green Peter and the other green men were amazed, and they rejoiced in what God had done. When green Peter returned home again, his other green friends asked him why he went to visit blue men. He told them that God had instructed him to do so, and he testified how blue men had changed color to green when the Holy Spirit of God moved upon them. When they heard that, they all began to rejoice and praise God.

From that day until now, green men and green women have been sharing with blue and orange men and women all over the world about the Plan of God. And wherever blue and orange people hear about and believe concerning God's Plan, a wonderful thing happens . . . they change from the color blue or the color orange to the color green. Faith is involved!!

Green Jesus said, *"I am the way, the truth and the life."* (John 14:6) He is the One who God has sent, and provided for men and women everywhere to be restored unto God and become His children. The Bible says that if you believe in your heart that God has risen up Jesus from the dead, then you shall be saved. It is the Plan of God. Faith is involved!

So . . . what color are you?

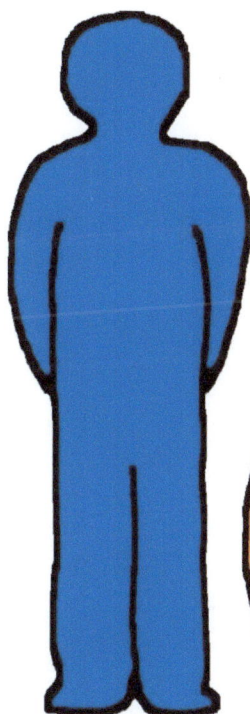

GENTILE

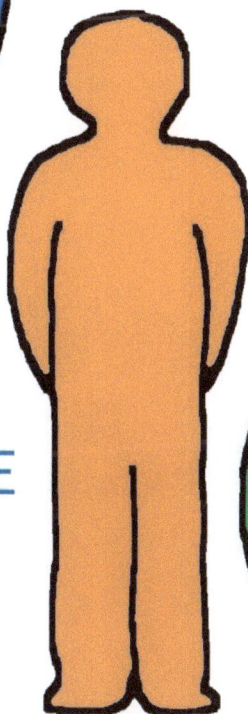

JEW

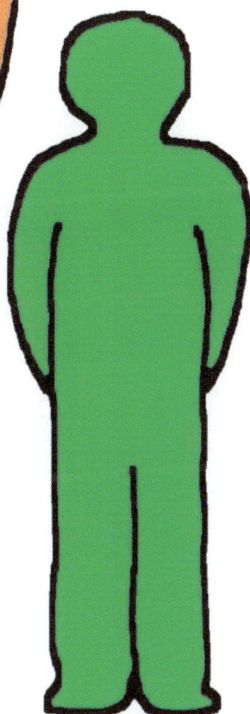

NEW
CREATURE

15

ADDENDUM

So, now that you know there are three different types of people in the world . . . Blue, Orange, and Green let's look a little closer to see just what it means to be a Gentile, or a Jew, or a New Creature in Christ.

What Does It Mean to be a Gentile?

At the beginning of God's creation of MAN, His intention was that all Human men and women should be His very own children . . . His family. Through the first couple, Adam, and Eve, God was going to get a whole entire race of *offspring*. Adam and Eve were His purposed prototype couple. They had been created _in_ His image. God had imparted a major portion of Himself to make them the type of creatures that they were. God class . . . **Not** God!! They would never be God, that was not even possible, but they were God class. Dwelling within the same existence category as God Himself. No other created creature had the privilege of being in that category. Angels were not created _in_ the image of God and _after_ His likeness. The creatures that today we know of as demons, before their fall, were not created _in_ His image and _after_ His likeness. And the animal kingdom was certainly not created _in_ the image of God. Only Man has that distinction. Only Man has the capacity to carry the very nature of God *(II Peter 1:4)*.

We can only hypothesize what the fullness of Adam and Eve might have been before they disobeyed God and fell from grace. But the Scripture says that God blessed them after their creation and commissioned them to go forth and to multiply. Had they been obedient to God and not transgressed, and multiplied as God had directed them, their children and their children's children, and their children's children's children would have all been born sinless. And today we potentially would be living in a *perfect world.* But that is not what happened is it?

When Sin entered into the picture again on this Earth, it brought about a change . . . an alteration. Adam and Eve were not the same as they had been before they disobeyed and fell from grace. That change had separated them from God. They were now distant. In fact, Sin's entrance actually had made them the step-children of the Devil himself. They now legally belonged to him. He was now their step-father and Sin was their task-master.

Now whenever they multiplied, the children that came forth were altered. They had a defiled Human/Sin nature. They were spiritually separated from God and it was going to take the very best that heaven had to give, to be able to finally deal with the Sin problem and make it possible for men and women to become the children of God again.

All of the people on this planet Earth, from the time of Adam and Eve, to the time of Abraham were Gentiles. No exceptions!

Being a Gentile means that a person does not have any legal standing before or with God.

There is no Covenant in place, no contract, no legal agreement between that individual and the Living God. It does not matter what color your skin is . . . nor what part of the world you are from . . . nor how good you are . . . nor how much money you have . . . nor how famous you are . . . nor what god you choose to worship. If you are not in a Covenant relationship with the Living God, the One True God, Yahweh, Jehovah . . . then you are a GENTILE.

What Does It Mean to be a Jew?

The word *Jew* is actually a slang term used for someone who is from the Hebrew tribe of Judah, of the Nation of Israel. The nation was originally composed of twelve tribes and Judah stands out because of the man Jesus Christ of Nazareth, who finds his birth lineage within that tribe.

The Scriptures talk about the Hebrew people. The Scriptures also tell us that Abraham was the first Hebrew *(Genesis 14:13)*. That reality occurred when the Living God Jehovah approached a Gentile man named Abram one day, and asked him if he would like to enter into a Covenant bond with Him. Abram knew what a covenant was . . . he knew that all that belonged to him would automatically belong to God if he accepted God's invitation. And everything that belonged to God would be available to him. He knew that God was asking him to be His partner, and to represent Him here on this Earth. Abram did not hesitate very long. He accepted God's invitation, and when he did God told him he needed for him to move out of his father's house and go into a strange new land that God would show him.

God promised Abram that He would take care of him . . . and that He would protect him if someone tried to harm him . . . and that He would provide for him so that he really needed nothing . . . and that He would even multiply him exceedingly and make his offspring as numerous as the sands on the seashore.

God gave Abram instructions on preparing the *cutting of the covenant.* Abram secured the correct animals that were needed and prepared them as he had been instructed. And when it was all ready to go, he sat down and waited for God to show up. God's vision for this Covenant was far bigger than Abram's. God knew that this was the beginning of something that was going to be eternal. As the evening approached, God caused Abram to fall asleep, and He passed through the pieces of flesh and cut the Covenant bond with Himself on the behalf of men. God *credited* Abram for being one of the participants of the Covenant, and Abram's name was changed to Abraham. It is with this event that Abraham entered into a Blood Covenant with the Living God and became the first Hebrew.

Abraham begat a promised son named Isaac, who begat a promised son named Jacob, who begat twelve promised sons, who became the patriarchs of the twelve tribes that made up the Nation of Israel. The people, who have descended from Abraham, through the promises, have been called Hebrews or Israelites or Jews.

The summation is this:

A Jew is anyone who is descended from Abraham, through the promises and is in a Blood Covenant relationship with the Living God, even today.

That relationship is called the Abrahamic Covenant within the Scriptures. The Mosaic Law, or the Law of Moses, is the legal set of *guidelines* for behavioral modification that are given for operating within that Covenant relationship. Today, some people who are Jewish know about this Covenant and live their lives according to the *guidelines*. Some other people who are Jewish do not know about their heritage or about the *guidelines* that go with the Covenant relationship.

But God knows who all of the Abrahamic Covenant people are, and He is a faithful God. He still protects them . . . He still provides for them . . . He still watches over them and loves them. They are still His *Chosen People* and that will never change, according to the Word of God.

What Does It Mean to be a New Creature?

The Gentiles are the first and the oldest type of people on the Earth today. The Jews are the second and next oldest type of people on the planet . . . and the New Creations are the third and youngest type of people.

Jesus Christ of Nazareth is the real, historic, Hebrew person who was born of a young virgin girl within the country of Israel about two-thousand years ago. While he walked upon this Earth, he said that he was the promised Redeemer that God said that He would send for the whole world. He said that he was the Messiah that God had promised for the Nation of Israel. He said that he was actually the Son of God . . . and they killed him for what he said.

When God established the Covenant with Abraham, the main thrust of God's Plan was to deal with the Law of Sin that had come into existence so many millennia ago. In order to do this, He was going to have to provide an *offering* to pay the price that Sin demands.

First, He will need a representative for righteousness in the Earth . . . thus we have the Covenant with Abraham.

Secondly, He will need to establish a *sacrificial system* . . . so the Law of Moses is instituted with an animal *sacrifice system* to atone for transgressions

And finally, He will need the *perfect sacrifice* to complete the process. So, when the fullness of time finally comes, *(Galatians 4:4)* one of the Persons of the Godhead shall need to leave Heaven, and clothe Himself with a suit of flesh, and present himself as that faultless sacrifice.

When Jesus was born, and circumcised into the Nation of Israel, he was a Jewish individual. He walked upon this Earth as a Jewish individual. He ministered upon this Earth, to the Jewish people, as a Jewish individual. When the time came, he presented himself as the Jewish promised Messiah that had been promised to the Covenant people of the Living God. However, they refused to receive him. They said that they did not want him and that they did not believe that he was really the promised Messiah that he said that he was, and so they killed him.

When he died, he died as the Covenant sacrifice that had been prophesied in the Scriptures. He died as a child of Abraham. He died as a Jewish man. And when he died because he was the declared Lamb of God . . . and the absolute perfect sacrifice that was needed to deal with the Law of Sin . . . the file of necessary pre-death actions that needed to be accomplished to establish the Plan of Redemption for Mankind was marked fulfilled . . . and the case folder was shut.

When Jesus of Nazareth was raised up from the dead, he was **not** raised up as a resurrected Jewish man. He was **not** raised up as a *remodel* of the Jewish person that he was before he died. He was, in fact, miraculously raised up as a brand <u>New</u> <u>Creation</u>. He was the brand new prototype of a brand new species of Human Being that had never existed before his personal resurrection. He was the *"firstborn of many brethren"* that would follow him over the next two-thousand years *(Romans 8:29)*. God had done nothing less than a supernatural, creative, act in establishing this new species of Human Being. And that of course, is in addition to rising up a dead Human Being back to life.

With the resurrection of the New Creation Jesus of Nazareth from the dead, there are now three separate and distinct *types* of human persons on the Earth: the Gentile, and the Jew, and the New Creature.

To become a New Creature simply means that you have surrendered to God and are Born Again within your spirit.

It means that you believe that when Jesus went to the cross of Calvary, he did it for you . . . not just for the whole world, but for you personally. It means that you accept that the New Creation Jesus of Nazareth is your own personal Saviour, who is rescuing you from eternal separation from the loving God of all creation, and from certain destruction in Hell.

He paid, through his death, the exorbitant price that Sin demanded, that you and I could never pay. It is not a matter of being a good person . . . or of donating all of your money to a worthy cause . . . or of belonging to any particular religion . . . or of going to any particular church . . . or of being of any particular ethnical background . . . or of how intelligent that you may be. It is a matter of accepting the redemption that God has made available, in trusting in the New Creation Lord Jesus Christ of Nazareth for your salvation.

Before you were a New Creation, you may have been a Gentile. If you are not of Abraham's seed according to the flesh, then that is what you were.

Before you were a New Creation, you may have been a Jewish individual. If you were part of the Covenant Chosen People of God, and you can trace your lineage back to Abraham, through the promises, then that is what you were.

But . . . please hear me! If you have trusted the New Creation Lord Jesus Christ of Nazareth to be your personal Saviour . . . if you are Born Again within your spirit . . . then YOU ARE **NOT** A GENTILE INDIVIDUAL ANYMORE . . . YOU ARE **NOT** A JEWISH INDIVIDUAL ANYMORE!!!

Just as a woman cannot be <u>pregnant</u> and <u>not pregnant</u> at the same time . . . so a Human person cannot be a Gentile and a New Creature at the same time. One cannot be a Jewish individual and a New Creature at the same time. There is no Scriptural basis anywhere within the Bible for God creating Hybrids.

Now this author realizes that what is being said is not going to sit very well with many people, and in particular with those who call themselves *Messianic* Christians. But this author is not the one who is declaring this spiritual reality of truth. The Apostle Paul received much persecution in his day because he was telling the people that he ministered to this very same thing *(II Corinthians 5:17-18)*. Being a New Creature means just that . . . brand **NEW!** Not a remodel of the old, but rather all things brand-spanking new. People, in general, have a difficult time letting go of certain things . . . particularly when it comes to things that they truly believe in down deep within their being. But letting go is just what we are going to have to do. By being a New Creature, we do not belong to the *belief system* that we once belonged to any longer . . . whether that is some pagan Gentile belief system, or whether that is the Jewish faith and the familiarities of the Law of Moses. And the whole of the Apostle Paul's writings tell us this very fact and encourage us to let go of the old and reach forth and embrace the new. We are to grab hold of all of the promises of God that are *in Christ* . . . Amen!

If what this author has just shared with you is new to your thinking, please consider the statement that the Apostle Paul made to the Christian believers in Galatia, in chapter two and verse eighteen, where he is touching upon this very concept.

"For if I build again, the things which once I destroyed, (by putting my trust in Christ) I make myself a transgressor." (Galatians 2:18; Enhanced)

Also, please understand that this is an inexhaustible subject. We would not be able to do this topic sufficient justice in this little book.

But we want to encourage and exhort you to look into the New Testament a little closer yourself, particularly the epistles that were written by the Apostle Paul. He and he alone has received a direct revelation of what really took place upon the resurrection of Jesus . . . from the New Creation Jesus himself. Take the time to set aside preconceived ideas and see what the New Testament really does say. We pray God's abundant grace abound toward you as you do.

Maranatha!

Meet the Author

By-The-Book Ministries, Inc. began in 2001 as a teaching outreach. Rob E. Daley has been gifted by God to be able to explain biblical truths in an easy to understand manner.

Many have been blessed by his teaching style.

Rob was saved and filled with the Holy Spirit in 1978 and has been instructed by the greatest teacher of all—the Spirit of Truth Himself. Rob is an ordained minister with the Assemblies of God International Fellowship and has pastored in various churches over the past 34 years.

It is the desire of this ministry to see the body of Christ solidly taught, and grow up into the things of the Lord. Rob is available for seminars, retreats, conventions, etc.

Rob can be reached at:

thedaleys@bythebookministries.org

http://robdaleyauthor.com

www.ingramcontent.com/pod-product-compliance
Lightning Source LLC
Chambersburg PA
CBHW041759040426
42447CB00001B/21